The Dedicated Ex-Prisoner's Guide to Life and Success on the Outside

10 Rules for Making It in Society After Doing Time

The Dedicated Ex-Prisoner's Guide to Life and Success on the Outside

10 Rules For Making It in Society After Doing Time

Richard Bovan

This book was printed in the United States of America.

ISBN 0-9792953-3-5   978-0-9792953-3-1

Library of Congress Control Number: 2009935348

First Edition

This book can be purchased in bulk via the following distributors: Ingram, Baker & Taylor, Barnes & Noble, Amazon.com (U.S., U.K., & Canada) and Bertrams

Also available online at WWW.FULLSURFACEPUBLISHING.COM

Dedications

I would like to dedicate this work to my entire family. You guys believed in me when I didn't believe in myself, and for that I will forever be grateful.

The Rules

✦ • • • • • • • • ◆ • • • • • • • • ✦

The Rules

◆—◆—◆

"It does not matter what you are trying to accomplish; it's all a matter of discipline."

Wilma Rudolph, 1940-1994
American Three-time Olympic Gold Medalist
Track & Field

"You never really know just how strong you are...until being strong is the only option you have left."

Anonymous

Change, Change, Change is What It's All About

One of the most profound challenges facing America as well as many other nations is dealing with the reintegration of multitudes of ex-prisoners who have been convicted of crimes and sentenced to serve some time inside prison or jail and who have served that time and been released. Right now there are more people incarcerated all over the world than at any other time in recorded history. America itself has more than 25% of the world's prisoners though its population only makes up about 5% of the world's people. Though this is the reality, the fact remains that the overwhelming majority of people that are sent to do time eventually are released and are (supposedly) expected to reenter mainstream society and become productive citizens. The problem with this "expectation" is that many times it is rendered somewhat unrealistic due to 2 things: the non-progressive social policies of many governments and nations regarding ex-prisoners, and the lack of knowledge and understanding on the part of many ex-prisoners of what exactly it will take (under the circumstances) in order for them to in fact become that productive law-abiding citizen that he or she is expected to be and formerly may not have been. This guidebook will deal with both these issues but will mainly focus on the second one.

Some folks say that the hardest thing in the world for us human beings to do is to change. That's not talking about people changing things in the world or people changing their minds about something or anything like that; but people changing themselves. To effectively and fundamentally change who you are involves changing your perceptions, your belief systems, your fraternizations, your habits and your actions. My own personal experiences have shown me that it is especially hard for someone who has spent time in prison to change; it's more of a process, more of a challenge and the odds are definitely more against you if you've been engaged in living a criminal lifestyle, been convicted and incarcerated and spent significant time away from society. After serving over a decade in prison myself and then subsequently being faced with the real life choice of either changing or perishing, I'm convinced that though changing oneself is definitely not an easy process or accomplishment for ex-prisoners and ex-criminals I know that real change *is* possible and it is definitely a necessary component to being able to survive and sustain oneself after being incarcerated and released back into society. I've successfully done it (knock on wood) and I know of many others that have also done it in spite of the odds, society, and everything else that stood in our way.

It goes without saying that it's not just in the best interest of the ex-prisoner or ex-convicted criminal to change for the better; it's in every citizen's best interest and it's also a matter of public safety. I would like to think that most reasonable people realize this and I don't think that most people in society should prefer that released ex-criminals return to their neighborhoods and communities worse off than they were when they went into prison. In America, over 700,000 people are released from prisons and jails every year with about 75% of them returning to lockup within the first 3 years. (In most other nations, the rearrest and return-to-prison rates for ex-prisoners are lower than 75% but are still extremely high.) This long-present reality has been termed "the revolving door" because it seems for many ex-prisoners that once they have been incarcerated they will be incarcerated again and again in their lifetimes, and therein lies the real issue at hand: Recidivism. How to effectively curb recidivism has become a much discussed topic when it comes to prison reform, though I must say that so far there has only been, at best, a lackluster effort to effectively address it and turn things around, policy-wise. Therefore, it still remains the case that most of those released from prison are not sufficiently "rehabilitated" nor afforded many opportunities and thus do predictably end up returning to prison within very short time spans.

Though I am an American-born male and though most prisoners and ex-prisoners are male in pretty much every societal demographic, this guide is written for any and all persons, male or female, black, white, Asian, Latino, Jewish, Indian, etc., not just in America but anywhere in the world who are currently incarcerated or who has ever spent significant time in prison or jail and who wants to reenter society as a forward thinking, functional, law-abiding citizen. I believe that there are many fundamental commonalities that come with incarceration and reentry that for the most part transcends national and international boundaries, gender and race. I also believe that there is a meld of some very complex but also some very simple things that a person newly released from prison can do to greatly improve his or her chances of sustaining themselves and their family once they are out and back in society. In most countries, ex-felons and those who have been to prison are not exactly welcomed back into society with open arms or allotted the same rights and opportunities that they had before their conviction and incarceration but nevertheless must find ways to function and survive within that society. For that reason, among others, it will definitely be necessary for most ex-prisoners to change many things in their lives, minds, and personal environments.

It is my honest opinion that if given the chance most ex-prisoners, not all of course, would choose to be at least marginal law-abiding citizens and not do anything criminally serious enough to land them back in prison. As I've said, I spent over 10 years in prison myself and I've known hundreds if not thousands of people just like me and I can say with all honesty that I have never met an ex-prisoner who had done substantial time inside prison who wanted to be back locked up. I have, however, come across countless prisoners and ex-prisoners who did not have a realistic, general understanding of what to do to make their reentry into society as painless and as successful as possible under the circumstances. That was my purpose for putting this guide together; to list and explain 10 general "rules" that will apply to most if not all ex-prisoners on how to best do that. The Rules and suggestions offered in this guide are, in my opinion, the most positive and proven ways for ex-prisoners to prevent themselves from going back to prison and also gives some insight from an ex-prisoner's perspective on how to not only survive on the outside but how to thrive in society as well.

I wanted to keep this guidebook as readable, short and concise as possible so that everyone, no matter their educational level, that needs and wants to can read and understand it, and in a timely manner. There are many other books, guides and manuals that have been published about reentry and recidivism and some are very useful but many of them are super-lengthy and only a few are written by actual ex-prisoners, which I think in a way is partly the source of the recidivism problems in many respects; so many of the policy-makers, legislators and other movers and shakers in the criminal justice field take their cues from these non-experience based writings. Idealism and real life experiences are 2 totally different things and I generally think that when people offer up suggestions and specifics on how to do something they should not just be marginally experienced or "educated" on the subject they're talking about but if at all possible they should have lived and experienced it firsthand. When a person lives or has lived what they claim expertise on, it gives them a clarity that can hardly be replicated or substituted. I have indeed lived and experienced everything that is suggested in the 10 Rules myself, as have many other successful ex-prisoners, and I know for a fact that the advice and information offered in this guide is really what most ex-prisoners need to hear, know, and practice so that they will forever remain *ex*-prisoners.

★ Rule #1 ★

Don't Forget Where You Came From!

One thing's for sure: Being incarcerated, confined, imprisoned, jailed, locked down, whatever you want to call it, is one of the worst unnatural predicaments that any human being could ever have to endure in life next to physical torture, and many folks even consider death to be preferable to long-term incarceration. Personally, I myself feel that I would rather die than have to go and do significant prison time again after having served over 10 years in prison on my first (and last) conviction. For me, being locked up was such a traumatic and undesirable experience that it even made me decide that never again would I own a pet animal that I had to keep locked inside of a cage or hooked up on a chain; that's how serious and deep of an affect being incarcerated had on me. I absolutely hated not being free. I hated being told what to do all of the time. I hated having to work hard everyday for pennies. Most of all, I hated being away from my family and hated seeing how my being in prison affected them. That "hate" for my life circumstances while I was incarcerated was a major impetus for me wanting to change my life so badly; I had definitely decided that the very last thing I wanted was to have to ever go back to prison and do more time.

Typically this is how it goes: When ex-prisoners first come home, especially if it's after a long period of imprisonment, they instinctively feel that the worst part of the whole ordeal is over. You will feel like you have finally arrived at the light at the end of the tunnel and that most of your worries and problems are a thing of the past. Things may even seem easy for you at first, like in the first few weeks of your release. Soon after, the true reality of the situation sets in and completely shatters that temporary emotional high you're enjoying and you then realize that you are really behind the 8-ball; you have to make some real fast decisions on how you will take care of yourself and handle your obligations. This part of the transition can be very trying for any ex-prisoner and it is at this very critical stage that all kinds of problems, issues and challenges usually begin to present themselves.

The post-release scenario for the average ex-prisoner involves nearly every negative aspect possible with respect to family, environment, and securing gainful employment. For some ex-prisoners, the stress of that can be enough to make them just throw up their hands and say "I give up!" I myself cannot count the number of times that I had thoughts about giving up when I first got out; when anger, frustration, temptation, desperation, and neediness set in they are a dangerous combination and can make any human being momentarily think irrationally. However, I wholeheartedly suggest that when or if ever ex-prisoners feel those same feelings that they do what I made it a point to do when I felt them; sit down, take a few deep breaths, and remember where you just came from. I mean really make it a point to flashback to those days when you were locked down and all the stuff that came with it and then consciously ask yourself the question "Would I rather go back to that life?" because for the most part, all those negative feelings and thoughts, if you allow them to, will be what induces you to do something (or not do something) that very well may land you back in prison.

I am of the belief that if a person can endure being locked up and literally living in a cage for a substantial amount of time, living in very close quarters with only members of your same sex, some of whom may not be the best of roommates and neighbors, and accept being told what to do on a daily basis; when to eat, when to work, when to use the phone to talk to your loved ones, when to watch television, when to sleep, when to wake up, when to shower and even when to speak, then that person surely can endure and make it through whatever challenges the free world presents. I believe that anyone who has ever been locked down for any significant amount of time and made it out with a sane mind and sound body can definitely handle *anything* after that, but ex-prisoners have to consciously take on and maintain that same mentality themselves once they are out of prison, preferably before even getting out.

Of course, that's not in any way meant to suggest that maintaining that mentality will be an easy thing to do on the outside. One notion I will consistently reinforce and reiterate throughout this guidebook: **Nothing will come easy for the ex-prisoner.** It will most definitely be an arduous task for most but I believe that adversity doesn't make a person who they are; it just reveals who they *really* are on the inside. And like they say, what doesn't kill you makes you stronger. So as I've said, I believe that anyone who has already made it out of prison with a sane mind and sound body is capable of enduring mostly anything if they remain focused and put forth the necessary effort, and in doing that I know that it will definitely be worthwhile to every now and again take some time to reminisce about all of the negativity that you left behind when you got out of prison and use that memory as strong motivation, as I and many other successful ex-prisoners do, to do whatever it takes and endure whatever you may have to endure in order to remain free. It will be especially useful to remember this particular piece of advice if you are on parole or probation when you are released. Remember: As long as you are free, anything can happen and unforeseen positive opportunities at least have the chance to present themselves and could very well manifest into God knows what, but if you are incarcerated there is little to no chance that any positive opportunity will come your way while you're in there.

There is a popular cliché that goes "A man cannot move forward while looking back" and while that may be true in the purest sense of the meaning behind it, it is just as true, especially when it comes to the reentry of ex-prisoners into society, that you can never afford to forget, even for a minute, where you came from. Though some of the memories and experiences of prison may very well be super duper negative or something you don't have any desire to relive or think about, I really do think that most ex-prisoners who end up going back to prison have that, among other things, in common; they did not make it a point to periodically reflect, especially during the hardest and most stressful of times, on what all they went through while they were locked down. Those ex-prisoners that are really serious about getting out and staying out of prison should take care not to make that same mistake.

★ Rule #2 ★

Change Your Former Playgrounds, Playmates and Playthings

I speak from personal experience when I say that being released from prison even after a short period of time but especially after a long period of incarceration is one of the most euphoric and spirit-lifting experiences that any human being could ever have. When I first came home from prison I felt like a brand new man, a brand new creature even...like a gigantic boulder had all of a sudden been lifted from my shoulders. It's a feeling that is really almost indescribable. As was pointed out in Rule #1, while incarcerated most folks spend lots of time dreaming of the day that they will be released and many times those thoughts and dreams about coming home from prison are based more on fantasy than on that person's actual reality that they will be facing once they are out on the streets and back in society.

As a result, most of those getting out of prison will find that the homecoming celebration for them will be very short-lived indeed. When you first come home there indeed may be a celebrational attitude flowing around and your old acquaintances may seem very glad to see you free again and some of them may very well be truly happy for you. Yet and still, it's almost certain that for most ex-prisoners some of those very same associates, friends, and even family members contributed to your former criminal mentality and negligent actions in some way. I have found that in most cases where a person has a habit, whether it be a good or bad habit, that there is usually some sort of support system around them that enables them to maintain that habit; that is just as true for people with drug habits and addictions and other bad habits as it is for people with more progressive and productive habits like reading or exercising. Being "criminal minded" in my opinion is also a habit, hence the term "habitual criminal" that is used in U.S. sentencing laws and courts to describe those that attain multiple felony arrests and convictions.

The old saying "No Man is an Island" is very, very true. Human beings are social creatures and we need some kind of external support in whatever we endeavor upon, good or bad, and especially so when it involves changing one's thinking and behavior. Since our thoughts determine our actions and our actions determine our habits and our habits heavily determine our life circumstances, the lifestyle patterns that we develop are definitely very instrumental in how far we get (or don't get) in life. When we find ourselves repeatedly engaging in negativity many times it's the environment, meaning the totality of the people, places and things that we choose to put energy into and pull energy from, that is a major part of the problem.

That being said, it is almost always necessary for ex-prisoners who are serious about staying out of prison to change/replace their old playgrounds, playmates and playthings once they are out of prison; which means changing their environment, some of their personal associations, as well as many of the physical and non-physical things that they were most interested in. For most all ex-prisoners, these 3 categories of things are the main "triggers" for their criminal mentality and behavior, and each individual must clearly identify and define them as such within their own mind. **To become successful after being incarcerated you will have to *un*-become a**

Change Your Former Playgrounds, Playmates and Playthings

product of your old environment and associations and interests and become a product of a new environment and new associations and new interests, which will bring on the development of new habits and new ways of thinking and new and better interests and opportunities.

In most all societies, there are whole industries that exist where people get paid to "create" support systems for other people; in diet and exercise, in education and in business, in terms of motivational speaking, etc. Not the case for ex-prisoners; there really are not very many industries in existence that help ex-prisoners reintegrate once they are released back into society. In America, being on parole, probation or supervised release does not suffice either because they are typically enforced or carried out in a punitive fashion and not a rehabilitative fashion and are not set up as a way to help provide ex-prisoners with the much needed motivational advice, resources, opportunities, etc. in order to best facilitate the transition from prison to freedom (not even the typical halfway house fits the bill since they are for-profit businesses that only have a very temporary presence in the ex-prisoner's situation). The motivation to change yourself and whatever else that needs to be changed in your life really has to come from within your own mind and heart. For the most part, successful people in general are not wholly products of their environments but are moreso products of their decisions within whatever environment, which is why it is so important for you to *decide* to change or replace everything in your life that has been having a negative affect on you and your wellbeing. There are countless examples of ex-prisoners getting out of prison and returning to their old stomping grounds and reacquainting with their old affiliates and retaining their old habits and ending up going right back to their old prison because of it.

Of course not everyone has the ability to physically relocate or totally distance themselves geographically from their old neighborhood or community. In cases like this, the ex-prisoner just has to maintain a higher level of focus than those who do have the ability to relocate. Though it is definitely a positive and tremendously helpful thing to relocate when necessary and possible, you can still do what you need to do in order to maintain your freedom if you can't; not everybody that lives in less than desirable areas or around negativity chooses to engage in criminal activity. For those that want to relocate but cannot for whatever reason, just remember that if ever you find yourself in a compromising situation due to where you are, you may just have to deal with it, suck it up, and maintain your focus until you can do better. Even still, in that situation you can be in the process of developing and working toward a plan to eventually relocate and at the same time be a positive influence and have a positive affect within your current environment by doing the right thing and taking care of business in spite of whatever negativity is present.

All in all, it is extremely important that you as an ex-prisoner know that you must abandon all of the past negative associations, connections, problems, vendettas and grudges of your former life in order to move on to bigger and better things and a brighter future for yourself on the outside. Of course, for you to truly be able to erase these negative presences in your life requires *you* to change yourself *first*; changing your playgrounds, playmates and playthings can only be effective after you have done that. Then, you will be able to positively move forward into the future because you have let go and risen above your past; the same past that almost certainly had lots to do with you going to prison in the first place.

★ Rule #3 ★

Do Not See Criminal Activity as an Option

When I was released from prison in 2004, I worked for a friend of mine's construction company while I was still in the halfway house. Before I was even able to fully complete my 6 month halfway house term I was forced to leave that job because of financial issues he and his business were having, so in just a few months after being released and after having served over 10 years straight I found myself facing not only unemployment but also unexpected family issues due to the job loss; when I had gotten out of prison I was immediately put on child support by the mother of my daughter and when I lost my job that meant that I couldn't keep up with my monthly payments. Of course I had immediately started to try and find other employment so that I could keep providing for my daughter and paying my halfway house fees but before I knew it weeks had gone by and then came the threat of being sent back to prison if I didn't find another job within a short time frame, per halfway house rules. This was probably one of my most trying time periods since I've been out of prison, and I will admit that it is definitely easier in theory to remain motivated and focused in these types of extremely stressful situations than it is to actually do it in real life. Like what was also spoken on in Rule #1, it is at times like these that desperation and temptation are at their highest levels and if you aren't careful you just might consider reverting back to your old criminal activity of choice in order to stave off the situation. It is also at times like these that ex-prisoners need to especially apply Rules #1, #2 and #3 of this guide; in addition to the first 2 Rules, you must learn to do what I did: not see *any* criminal activity, no matter how potentially lucrative or beneficial it may seem to be, as an option.

A no-nonsense determination to cease and desist from crime and criminal activity of any kind, no matter what, is the ideal and only applicable mindset for any ex-offender who does truly desire to not only maintain his or her freedom but be progressive in society as well. That means, for you, no illegal drug using or drug dealing. That means no possessing of weapons and no breaking of any probationary rules. That means absolutely no fraternizing with those who are into criminal activity when you can help it. That means taking great precautions to not break the laws of the land or even ever being charged again with any sort of crime, and not just for self-interest reasons but for moral reasons as well; begin to try to make a habit of doing what's right *because* it's right. Having that no-nonsense determination also means taking pretty much everything in life just a little more seriously than everyone else around you does because your life circumstances as an ex-prisoner are most likely more serious than most other folk's (who aren't ex-prisoners) life circumstances. Like many other pieces of advice offered in this guide, it is really best if you soon to be ex-prisoners who are currently in prison can come to these very important realizations and have them deeply set within your minds even before being released...that way you will already be ahead of the game when you first step foot out and when/if hard times hit or when you are presented with challenges and temptations upon your release, because some of those challenges and temptations may very well come just days or even hours after you get out.

As an ex-prisoner, when you walked out of the jail or prison you were released from you were already a marked man/woman. In most societies and especially in America and in the West, many folks really do seem to expect those who have served time in prison to do something else criminal and eventually return to prison, and of course most do and that's primarily because those who have felony criminal records or who have spent years in prison are systematically frozen out of many opportunities and availabilities that are afforded to the average everyday citizen who has never been incarcerated or does not have that criminal record. Everyone knows that it is extremely difficult for ex-prisoners to find and maintain gainful employment and that we are denied access to "the system" when it comes to employment, housing, socioeconomic programs for the poor, and even voting. From the perspective of most ex-prisoners, this reality amounts to them being basically de-citizenized via unnecessary discrimination and extra punishment. If you ask me, making it so difficult for so many ex-prisoners to succeed is tantamount to jeopardizing public safety. There should be such a thing as truly "paying off your debt to society" if you are indeed released from prison and you've served and completed your sentence and your probation/parole/supervised release, but that is not what the reality is for ex-prisoners all too often.

Nevertheless, those who do have criminal records and who have done time must still survive and find legitimate ways to achieve their goals amidst the built-in obstacles that societies and governments have in place; illegal activity as a way to obtain things or achieve goals simply cannot be seen as an option for ex-prisoners who are dedicated to change and continued freedom. (Along with the forestated general reasons for not engaging in criminal activity, you also know that incurring repeated criminal charges and convictions brings stiffer penalties with every new time. Unless you really don't mind going back to prison and probably for a longer period of time than you've previously served [depending on the charge and conviction and your criminal record] you should steer wide and clear from criminal activity. Committing more criminal acts and engaging in a criminal lifestyle almost assures that you will eventually get caught and go back.)

In prisons there are sometimes efforts made on the part of some of the prison staff or government programs to induce "rehabilitation" within prisoners and soon to be ex-prisoners but those efforts usually only go so far, somewhat like the efforts systematically put forth by the probation and parole offices and halfway houses in the U.S. (In America, over the last number of years those in-prison rehabilitative programs and efforts have been either totally eliminated or severely decreased while the laws and regulations that serve to diminish the rights and privileges of ex-prisoners have been consistently expanding in free society.) But, as I've said, despite any external efforts or provided rehabilitative tools it still remains true that real and genuine rehabilitation comes only from within the decisive mind and heart of the individual person and I think that a clear sign of someone being truly rehabilitated is when, despite whatever circumstances or hardships they may be facing, they no longer consider criminal activity to be a viable option for their livelihood. It comes with the individual person finally coming to the realization for him or herself that lawbreaking and committing crime is not only morally wrong and bad for society but that it doesn't pay; that it doesn't pay for the overwhelming majority of people in the world and that it definitely doesn't pay for the ex-prisoner...and then acting on that realization on an hourly, daily, weekly, monthly, yearly, and lifetime basis.

⋆ Rule #4 ⋆

Take Full Responsibility For Your Actions; See Yourself as the One to Blame For Whatever Happens to You

"Personal Responsibility! Personal Responsibility! Everyone should take personal responsibility for their own actions!" is the neo-social battle cry for the new millennium it seems. From politicians to pundits to civil rights leaders to even slews of substance abuse and behavior related reality T.V. shows, everyone seems to be decrying the fact that many folks blame others for problems and issues that they themselves are really mainly responsible for. My own message about personal responsibility is not as general as that because I do understand that sometimes a person is not necessarily responsible for, or in total control of, everything that happens to them in life. However, at the same time I also believe that every person should understand and act upon the fact that we humans are indeed in control of a large part of what happens to us and that in understanding that fact and applying ourselves to that principle we do utilize our maximum amount of control over our own lives. For ex-prisoners who want to maintain their freedom and succeed in society, it is an absolute must that you think in terms of yourself being responsible for what happens to you. Doing this is not only "taking responsibility" but it is also employing a certain self-controlling mentality that consistently considers the endgame consequences to whatever actions you may decide to take in any given situation; that particular aspect of it is what's most important for ex-prisoners.

I remember when in the infamous American prison drama film *Shawshank Redemption* the character Red, played my Morgan Freeman, was trying to show Andy Dufresne, played by Tim Robbins, that most of the other men in their penitentiary did not believe that they were responsible for their being locked up. When Red asked several prisoners what they were in for, their lightning fast response was "Didn't do it!" or to say that someone or something else was responsible for them being there. That scene depicted a notion that is really very true and typical with respect to many real life prisoners who do not understand the relationship between that particular way of thinking and them ending up being incarcerated in the first place. While doing my own time in prison, I rarely ran across men who rightly and admittedly saw themselves or their behavior as the main reason why they were incarcerated and for a long time I did not blame myself for me being incarcerated. **A common characteristic of criminal thinking is when a person does not see themselves and their own actions clearly and blames outside persons and circumstances for the outcome of their situation.** What we don't usually understand is that thinking like that is really what's at the core of many of our problems and that if we just changed that thinking around we could eliminate much of what needs to be eliminated from our lives and therefore create a better and more progressive reality for ourselves.

It's important to understand that you and only you are in control of *your* actions. Things may happen around you or even to you and yes; it's impossible to control everything that goes on around you but you can definitely control how you react to it. Many times it is our reactions to situations and circumstances that cause us to do something that is criminally wrong and/or that will come back to haunt us in some bad way. Any situation that involves choice or decision making on your part means that you and only you are responsible for whatever the outcome is. For ex-prisoners, it really is all about understanding and employing self-responsibility and self-discipline and therefore not being persuaded by or submissive to whatever negativity or hardships you may encounter. It is absolutely essential for the sake of not falling victim to circumstances that could send you back to prison that you see yourself as the sole person that is to blame for whatever happens to you where choice is involved once you get out of prison and maintain that way of thinking so that you will stay out of prison.

When we accept and bring personal accountability into our lives, it enriches us and we live more mindfully. We are more careful and we tend to make better decisions and do our best at whatever we engage in. When we take responsibility for our own actions and thus whatever happens to us, we are more aware, as we as ex-prisoners definitely need to be. As an ex-prisoner, you really can never be too aware and it has been said about many a successful ex-prisoner that they acted somewhat paranoid when it came to doing certain things, going certain places, and being around certain people. I do believe that paranoia is the highest state of awareness (if you don't believe me, walk out of your house and try to sneak up on a bird; you will not be able to do it because the bird is paranoid and always on the lookout for what could potentially harm it) and while I'm not suggesting that ex-prisoners literally need to be walking around paranoid all the time I am suggesting however, like what was said in the previous chapter, that you always try to maintain a high level of awareness of your own surroundings and actions and the actions of those around you and take it very, very seriously. This is an aspect of "taking responsibility" that ex-prisoners really cannot afford to ever ignore, not even for a minute; the 1 time you ignore it could very well be the time that you find yourself in some kind of hot water again.

All in all, real freedom comes with being responsible for your own life and seeing it as such; anything less that that is not real freedom. After experiencing the direct opposite of freedom while you were in prison, don't you want to truly taste freedom? Don't you want to be the one in charge of what happens or doesn't happen to you from now on? Well, the only way to do this is to fully embrace the notion of "I am the one responsible" and place yourself in the most powerful position that you can place yourself, which is the position of head decision maker and final authority over your own life, and I guarantee you that once you have done this you will immediately start to see better results across the board. I have learned to not give many guarantees in life, but that is one of the few guarantees that I can give with absolutely no fear of ever being proven wrong. I am convinced that there really is no other way for you the ex-prisoner, or anyone else for that matter, to pursue happiness and achieve success other than through embracing and enacting your own authority over your own life, and the way to do that begins with first seeing yourself as the one responsible for your life. After that, everything else will fall into place.

⋆ Rule #5 ⋆

Envision Your Own Path to Success; Have a Realistic Plan

Throughout this guidebook I reference some general things about the men and women that I know, and about myself as well, who have gotten out of prison and followed all the steps that are outlined in this guide and who are now successfully making it in society, but I think that everyone knows that we are currently the exceptions to the rule. As I previously pointed out in the Intro section, the recidivism or return to prison rate for ex-prisoners in America is about 75% within the first 3 years of release and probably somewhere around 85% or 90% within their lifetimes. I cannot count the number of men I personally know of that got out of prison, kind of started off well, then somewhere along the way backslid and went back to prison. Most of them went back for very simple and unnecessary stuff. I myself have not gone back again (and have no plans on ever doing so, knock on wood) and I can honestly say that it is largely because at a certain point I realized that it was totally, *totally* necessary that I develop and maintain for myself a realistic plan for how I would achieve my goals on the outside and then be determined to have the discipline to stick to it and carry it forward and make it happen. That's just what I did too, and that's what all success-minded ex-prisoners will need to do.

The minimum of what "success on the outside" means for the ex-prisoner or ex-convict is to legitimately be able to survive on the outside and not ever having to go back to prison...that's the *minimum*. Of course it could go well beyond that threshold; with proper planning, some opportunities, and hard work can come very high levels of contemporary success in many different areas. As far as planning, I think that the best time to start planning for what you are going to do on the outside is while you are still serving your time. Doing time in prison is pure wasted time unless *you* decide to use that time wisely, and as far as I'm concerned there is nothing wiser than planning for what you are going to do once you are out. In doing so, take care to make sure that your plan and ideas are doable and realistic but yet at the same time it's still okay to think and dream big, reason being I've never seen someone do something big or outstanding against great odds unless they first thought that they could do it. Make sure it's what *you* want to do, what you are good at or interested in, and try to learn and acquire whatever it is that you would need in order to bring that plan into fruition.

When I say make sure your plan is "realistic" I mostly mean that you should not plan to do too much too fast once you're out of prison and that you should take care to analyze every aspect of what it is you want to do and how you want to do it so as to not get taken by surprise by events you failed to plan for that could take you off course a little bit or prolong your success. Most times, it takes longer to complete things than we think and it is a chronic characteristic of human beings that we tend to underestimate the length of time it will take us to perform most tasks. This occurs mainly because we don't plan sufficiently, we set too many goals for too short a time span, and because we get distracted along the way. You must keep your focus on what your plan is and how you are going to go about implementing it and focus less on how long it may take for you to do it. Giving yourself mental time limits on achieving success could very well backfire and turn into a self-imposed mental trap that could potentially lead to negativity if things don't work out exactly the way you wanted in the time frame that you wanted...I've seen that happen to countless ex-prisoners as well. Coming out of prison, in regards to your plans and goals, you need to unequivocally be of a mindset that says no matter what it takes or how long it takes, you're staying the course.

To successfully reach a major goal, people need a reason to place that particular goal higher on their priority list than their other goals and aspirations and also need to be 100% dedicated to achieving that goal so that they will allocate their resources in the most efficient way. For ex-prisoners, that reason can be stated in 1 word: Freedom. There shouldn't be much room on your priority list for anything other than the things associated with you maintaining your freedom and surviving and being successful; everything else that would normally be a top priority for you, like the wellbeing of your family for instance, is inherently connected to you being free and successful anyway. Being successful *is* the goal of whatever plans you come up with, and while you are carrying out your plans it's definitely useful for you to always keep on the forefront of your mind that you cannot ever attain success while being locked up. As long as you can maintain your freedom, you have a chance at reaching your goals, whatever they may be.

Murphy's Law states "If anything can go wrong, it will" but I think "especially if you don't have a plan" should be added to that because failing to plan is essentially the same as planning to fail. Not having a plan is just simply not an option for those coming out of prison and jail; it really is almost the same as deliberately planning to fail. You need to have it formulated in your mind what you are going to do on the outside and you will need to be ready to not only take advantage of good opportunities that come your way but maybe even create some opportunities of your own. (With respect to this, Rules #6, #7, and #8 will delve into the need for ex-prisoners to focus on attacking and taking full advantage of any and all good opportunities that are externally presented to them as well as the great need for ex-prisoners to seek out ways to create their own opportunities and work hard to achieve them.) If you are reading this and you are incarcerated and you still have substantial time left to do on your sentence but will one day be getting out, just remember this: **Proper Preparation Prevents Poor Performance**, so unless you want to perform poorly out on the outside and risk getting sent back to lockup you had best get to preparing and planning right now if you haven't already. To ex-prisoners who are already out and those prisoners who will be released soon: Know that there are many ways of going forward but only 1 way of standing still—it is up to you to find your own particular way to move forward but once you do find it you definitely will need to go after it as if your life depended on it, because quite frankly, it does. My advice to you is that whatever you do decide to do, just make sure it is as well thought out as possible, realistic, and what you want. If you do that, you will be starting out on the narrow road that leads to success on the outside.

★ Rule #6 ★

Believe in Yourself; Don't Get Discouraged by Roadblocks and Hardships

We all know that everything in life has its limits. At some point, all people as well as all other living things reach the edge of what they can accomplish on talent alone or with minimal effort. At some point, no matter what it is that you are doing, if you do it long enough it will cease to become as easy as it was if it ever was easy; this is especially true when it comes to doing time and also when it comes to performing any kind of work. There are exceptions to most all rules of course, but this is one of those general life rules where there are few exceptions to it. For most folks, this point usually comes when they have tired of doing whatever it is they are doing and have lost the motivation to continue on with the same vigor and energy that they may have started out with, or when whatever they are doing has become too burdensome and/or painful. My point in bringing this up is this: For most ex-prisoners, I believe that this same invisible "threshold" for discomfort and hardship is naturally raised and made stronger by doing time and can become sort of like an extra psychological "tool" that can be really useful in hard times because as I've said, I believe that if a person can endure a substantial period of incarceration they can endure mostly anything if they put their mind to it.

Trust me when I tell you; I know how it feels to be broke with no job prospects on the horizon and no car and no support while having children to provide for, with bills piling high and frustration setting in. I have definitely been there. Most ex-prisoners have been there; it's really almost a certainty that there will be at least 1 period of time once you are out of prison, whether it be brief or prolonged, when you will be faced with this same scenario or one that is very similar to it. This is when you really will need to be self-motivated and strong in your decision to change your life around and beat the odds against ex-prisoners staying out and becoming successful.

There are 2 basic reasons why self-confidence and self-motivation are so important for the ex-prisoner. First off, ex-prisoners that really want to do something positive and exceptional once they are out will need to be self-motivated because there more than likely won't be many people around you who truly understand the ins and outs of your life circumstances and all that you are up against. It's sad to say, but you'll find that most folks won't really care about your situation period, much less understand it, and even your closest loved ones probably won't really understand everything dealing with all the restrictions and disallowances you face or the psychological affects that being incarcerated has had on you. Some of them, especially offspring and spouses and significant others, may even have unrealistic expectations of you...this sometimes happens with many ex-prisoners and when it does occur, if they aren't self-motivated and self-defined it can lead to them trying to live up to other's expectations and when they can't legitimately live up to those expectations they relapse back into criminal thinking and re-engage with criminal activity and end up back in prison again.

Secondly, in general, whenever anyone does something big or something that is "against the grain" of what everybody else is doing or expecting, they *have* to be self-motivated and possess lots of self-confidence. Being "average" is not an option for an ex-prisoner who wants to succeed because being average means going back to prison at some point, since most ex-prisoners do go back. Being extra-ordinary means just the opposite and extra-ordinary is what all successful ex-prisoners are, by necessity. You have to be able to think clearly for yourself and you must believe and have confidence in yourself. If you have self-confidence, you really have half the battle already won; like the old saying goes, "Confidence is Half the Battle". Once you're on the outside, you must have nearly the same mindset as a military soldier that is heading into a warzone in that you are expecting and prepared for hardships and conflict and confrontation but nevertheless are ready to do whatever it takes to come out of it the winner. In thinking like that, you are preparing yourself to not allow negative circumstances and/or scary situations to discourage you and take away your will to keep pushing on. Not being *dis*couraged means staying *en*couraged, and when you don't have the luxury of other people always being there to offer encouragement sometimes your own positive self-talk may be all the encouragement you may be able to receive at any given moment. Regardless of whatever the circumstance or situation, it's all about taking great care not to allow anything or anyone to rob you of your confidence and belief in yourself; the moment any ex-prisoner who desires success on the outside does that could very well be a moment he or she lives to regret.

Remember this: **In life, every setback is only a setup for a greater comeback**. Personally, I am a big advocate of the notion of faith. To me, having faith means steadfastly believing that something is possible even when it seems that it really isn't possible. I believe that faith is the cornerstone on which all great lives are built and all great deeds are achieved. When times get the hardest, it is our faith that sometimes helps us to maintain and persevere through it. Whether it be religion-based faith or just you having strong faith in yourself and your own abilities, I think that faith is an especially necessary ingredient for all human success that is attained against great odds. I'll say it again: As a rule, nothing comes easy for ex-prisoners so if you as an ex-prisoner are indeed ever successful it *will* be against great odds, so you *will* need some faith to help you overcome those odds.

Yes; you will need to change and take more responsibility for your life and actions. Yes; you will need a plan. Yes; you will need resources and opportunity. But moreso than anything else, you will need perseverance and you will need faith and belief in yourself. Suffice it to say, without those qualities ex-prisoners have very little chance of reaching real success (as defined in Rule #5) on the outside.

★ Rule #7 ★

Use Jobs as Stepping Stones; Focus on Entrepreneurship

Like I've previously stated, when I was released from prison after serving my time I was lucky enough to have a family friend that had his own business and was willing to hire me. Though I did stay on the job until I was let go by him, for the time I had the job it only paid just above minimum wage and after just a few months of working it I had already seen that there was no way I was going to be able to support my family and myself on that wage. After I was let go I found myself another temporary construction job that paid a little bit better. I stayed on that job for another 4 months then was let go again for no fault of my own. With losing that second job came the reality of being unemployed without being eligible for unemployment benefits since I had not been working long enough and had not earned enough money during the time that I was employed. At that point I decided to start my own business. I had known that my employment options were extremely limited from get-go. But that's what I did; I started my own business and threw myself headlong into it.

Since I had been working at my friend's business and the other job performing different types of services to homeowners for a few months (building construction, painting, laying tile floors, laying carpet, etc.) I had gotten a bird's eye glimpse of how to go about running that particular type of business plus I was very determined and knew that my back was against the wall and, since I was already on the bottom, that there was nowhere for me to go but up. I had also done some of that same type of work while I was in prison. So to put it in a nutshell, I did some extra preliminary research and then went and got myself a business license, some insurance, had my girlfriend print up some flyers and solicitational business material, got a few basic materials that I would need, and went at it hard and to date I have done pretty well for myself despite my status as an ex-felon. My point in reiterating this period in my own reentry here is this: When getting out of prison you will be bombarded with the notion of "get out and get a job" and told by many that if you just find a job and work hard and don't commit any more crimes that everything will be alright. Well, in this day and time nothing could be farther from the truth, as I myself quickly learned. For the ex-prisoner, decent paying jobs are not that easy to get and are even harder to keep if you are lucky enough to even get one, and for the overwhelming amount of available jobs in society the requirements are that you not only have some sort of college degree, some skills and some work history, but also that you have no criminal record. In America, many companies won't even hire you if you have a misdemeanor conviction on your record. In addition to that you have aspects of globalism, new technology, and businesses consolidating and merging that have severely decreased the demand for certain types of labor in many developed countries, and that is a fact. Discrimination and bad social policies and laws with regards to ex-prisoners are gigantic problems as well. In terms of bad social policies, there is a widespread generally accepted notion of "once a felon, always a felon" and it seems that for some reason mostly everyone caters to that belief and that's really a shame, to say the least.

Nevertheless, it *is* important for men and women who are getting out of prison to somehow find employment, especially when they are first getting out. There are many resourceful books that have been written specifically for ex-offenders dealing with all of the different concerns that come with that, a few of which are listed at the end of this guide. I strongly suggest that you read some of those types of books and do some independent research on what types of jobs are readily available for ex-prisoners and specifically find out which jobs are available in your own release residence area. (Also, in the U.S. especially, knowing about how the credit system works helps tremendously; you would be surprised how many people there are in society who have never been to prison but don't know how the credit system works. Most ex-prisoners who have done long stretches of time in prison come out with a clean slate credit-wise, not that they have good credit but that they don't have bad credit and can quickly have good credit if they play their cards right. Having good credit can definitely be of major benefit to you personally in terms of being able to acquire certain necessities and also as far as you being able to start your own business. And since credit scores are also being heavily used now by companies to determine whom they hire or don't hire, having a decent credit score can possibly aid in securing employment.)

The point of this chapter is not to provide you with specific detailed information on what exactly to do for yourself as far as anything entrepreneurial is concerned, since every person's situation is unique and what works for one person may not work for another. Whatever it is that you choose to do or that you are good at, you will have to do the research for yourself on what all you need to do in order to get your business started and make it work. The point of this chapter is to generally advise anyone that is coming out of prison to aspire to become entrepreneurs and not be of the mindset that a job is going to enable you to sustain yourself and your family. Yes there are exceptions to this rule but not many. As was the case with me when I came home, for most ex-prisoners the typical job wage that is readily attainable will not provide sufficient financial security over the long term. It will not provide certain much-needed benefits. It will normally not be the type of job that will have real stability associated with it. Most job occupations nowadays have no surety of tenure anyway, not even for those workers that are well-educated and well-qualified and who are not ex-prisoners. That is the hard fact of the matter.

Statistics clearly show that people who have been released from prison and who are earning a sufficient income are much more likely not to return to prison, so as far as I'm concerned the best chance that an ex-prisoner has of earning that sufficient income is by owning their own business. It's what worked for me, and that's why I *know* that entrepreneurship is the way to go. I don't know about you, but I didn't want to be continuously stressed out literally for the rest of my life worrying about keeping a backbreaking job that didn't pay me enough to live on and that may or may not be there tomorrow. To me, that sort of existence is too similar to actually being in prison, especially if you're not earning enough to sufficiently provide for your children. I think a lot of ex-prisoners really feel that way too, which is why so many get discouraged and become hopeless and end up doing something reckless that sends them back to prison when faced with that sort of reality, but the smart alternative is to plan to at some point start your own business and create your own financial stability for yourself and take the time to work towards that.

In today's world, I believe that it is not really far-fetched to imagine that men and women can come from incarceration and become entrepreneurs, in mass numbers even. Some folks may think it's not realistic, but that sort of negative thinking, if adhered to, would have kept all of the many great feats, discoveries, and accomplishments that have occurred throughout the history of the world from actually manifesting. As a particular point of interest, I would suggest that business-minded ex-prisoners look toward the Internet as a particularly useful platform; you can research, start and run a viable business using the Internet without much upfront cost and the best thing about Internet-based businesses from an ex-prisoner's point of view is that there is no one to ask you anything about your criminal history or do a background check. Most Internet-based businesses can easily be ran incognito by pretty much anyone and the benefits of the physical storefront of contemporary businesses minus all the costs associated with that can now be attained with a mere website. As an entrepreneur myself, the solicitational aspect of my own business is almost entirely Internet-based.

Men and women who are getting out of prison definitely have their backs against the wall economically speaking, there is no doubt about that, but we cannot afford to cry over spilled milk; we have to clean it up. I know that every single person coming out of prison cannot become an entrepreneur but I think that many can. Some of the smartest, strongest, and most creative people I have ever met in my life I met while I was serving my time in prison. I'm a big believer that if a person has the intelligence, is willing to put forth a strong effort, and has an opportunity afforded to them they will more than likely be successful in whatever they are trying to accomplish. For the ex-prisoner, the real task lies with having to self-educate and self-train sufficiently and having to create your own opportunities in most cases, but like so many ex-felons have shown, myself included, it is nowhere near impossible to do so. And like I said, I believe that if an average Joe like me can do it then anyone can do it. And just think: If enough ex-prisoners can become business owners, we can help change the trend of disenfranchising ex-prisoners by hiring other ex-prisoners to work for us! Fair treatment of ex-prisoners by the "system" and society *has* to be introduced to the mainstream in some kind of way or by some means, and it may just have to come by way of other ex-prisoners who have been able to achieve entrepreneurial success bringing the issue to the forefront, as myself and many others who are starkly opposed to ex-prisoner disenfranchisement are trying to do. By one way or another, it is necessary that one day things do change regarding ex-prisoner disenfranchisement because most ex-prisoners deserve, want, and desperately need a conventional chance to be able to legitimately sustain themselves and their families after they have finished paying their debt to society. Until that time comes, ex-prisoners should use jobs as stepping stones and focus on entrepreneurship.

★ Rule #8 ★

Be Ready and Willing to Work Harder than You've Ever Worked Before!

As has been previously pointed out within this guide, in making the transition from prison back to the free world you will definitely have to work harder and hustle harder at trying to accomplish the things you want and need to accomplish moreso than the average everyday citizen does, mostly because of your ex-felon/ex-prisoner status but also because of the time you have spent away from society, and this is especially true for those who have served long sentences. So the catch is to just expect that to be the case and to do all you can to be ready for it.

Most folks just in everyday life have to work hard and long hours for their pay. Since it is the current reality that ex-prisoners and ex-felons have many obstacles in their paths that the average person doesn't have, it really should be the expectation that you have that you will have to work much harder and apply much more dedication when it comes to achieving your goals. You can have the best plan in the world; even the best plan will stand absolutely no chance of becoming reality without hard work being applied. Like the saying goes, "The only place where success comes before work is in the dictionary." You can even be blessed enough to have a few extraordinary advantages working for you or you can think that you have some unique secret to success; still, nothing will work unless *you* do.

Hard work can be found to be something rewarding or it can be seen as something punishing. For ex-prisoners, I believe that if hard work on the outside is found to be rewarding it is more likely to aid in keeping them walking a straight line vs. committing crimes. If it is found to be punishing, then that may be used as a reason to see oneself as a victim and as an excuse to rekindle past criminal behavior. As an ex-prisoner who wants to be successful, you cannot be one of those people that equates hard work with punishment or suffering, even if you don't reap your desired benefits from your hard work for awhile. You have to fully welcome the idea of working hard and exercise patience when trying to reach your goals. As talked about in Rule #6, you cannot allow yourself to become disheartened by the fact that the effort required of you will be greater than most and that you may have to endure some extra undue pains in reaching them; you have to accept and embrace that reality. You cannot afford to become one of those folks that allows opportunity to pass you by because it looks like hard work either; many people let many an opportunity pass by and don't take advantage of them because they are afraid of the great effort that might be required of them but ex-prisoners cannot afford to be like that. To be successful on the outside, you have to be thinking in such a way that you *welcome* putting in that potentially tiresome and painful effort...after all, effort is only really effort when it begins to hurt anyway, right?

And as I've said, those serving time should expect this and thus prepare for having to put forth that extra effort once they get out even before they get out. While I was doing my own time in prison, I purposefully developed a mindset whereas I taught myself to deal with all the uncomfortableness and hardships of prison life by seeing it as mental practice for what I would face out on the outside. I also used that same mental tactic while I was on probation. This "practice" helped me get through some very difficult times while I was in prison and on probation and was eventually very useful in helping me to deal with having to work extra hard at not only making a living on the outside but also at maintaining my composure under pressure and walking a straight line and staying out of trouble. I would suggest that other soon-to-be released prisoners and ex-prisoners try the same thing, being that you have to deal with the reality that you have to deal with whether you like it or not, plus you do become better at any given thing when you have a chance to practice it. **Use your prison and/or probation time to practice dealing with the reality that will be forthcoming once you are released and free and clear of the penal system.** The axiom "Proper Preparation Prevents Poor Performance" doesn't just apply to Rule #5; it applies here too and is just another way of saying "Practice Makes Perfect".

High ambition is not something ex-prisoners are expected to have because of the great odds against us and the sparse opportunities provided to us by society but as I've stated, there is nothing that hard work and intensified focus cannot achieve. I believe that if you give a 100% effort all the time, somehow things work out in the end. The question is: Are you ready, willing and able to apply that necessary level of hard work and focus that will be necessary to compensate for all of what is not in your favor due to your ex-prisoner status? An analogy I like to use in reference to this is about how most handicapped people tend to overdevelop in the areas where they aren't hindered by their ailment in order to compensate for their shortcomings; people without eyesight usually learn to use their senses of hearing and smelling better than average folks, people without the use of their legs tend to develop stronger arms because they have to use them more than they normally would have, people with certain learning disabilities sometimes have or develop other extra-ordinary capabilities, etc...this is essentially the same thing that ex-prisoners have to do. Ex-prisoners have to overdevelop their "hustle muscle" to compensate for all the other things that they don't have going for them. To use another analogy, I liken the pathway to success for most ex-prisoners as being able to swim *against* the current in a swimming race where everyone else is swimming *with* the current and yet still cross the finish line, just not in first place, obviously. For ex-prisoners to break the odds and successfully "swim against the current" means that while you may not have started off when everyone else did and had all kinds of extra things working against you, you still finished and successfully completed the race and still got to where everyone else in the race was. It also means that you would have to be stronger and more focused than the others in the race too. I know that not every person possesses that level of strength or focus ability but as I've said, some of the most creative, intelligent and definitely some of strongest people that I have ever met in my life I met while I was in prison. I'm convinced that with redirected focus, some renewed self-determination, some opportunity and some hard work that many of those that are incarcerated can succeed even beyond their own imaginations.

Remember: The race is not always won by the fastest but *is* always won by the one who endures to the end. Ex-prisoners who are ready and willing to work hard for what they want can definitely still finish "the race" as winners.

★ Rule #9 ★

Stay Close to Those Who Truly Care For You; Be Family-Oriented

Like having the ability to earn a decent living, having positive personal relationships plays a central role in decreasing recidivism as well, and all the statistical research I have ever seen suggests that ex-prisoners who have stable personal relationships have a much greater chance of succeeding on the outside than those who do not. My own personal experiences and observations concur with those findings as well. The Rules in this guidebook are focused on ex-prisoners making mentality and lifestyle changes and explaining certain aspects about how best to do it under the current world circumstances and why it's worthwhile to do it; having someone other than yourself that makes undertaking that hard task of changing worthwhile and easier is very important to the process. Most times that "someone" will either be your offspring, your wife or husband or significant other, your siblings or other family members and/or true friends, or any combination of all or any of them.

Being a former criminal myself and being someone who personally knows scores and scores of other former and current criminals from all over the world and from every ethnic and social background, I know that criminal behavior is sometimes subconsciously used as a way of filling a void or emptiness in a person's life. Sometimes a lack of self-confidence combined with feelings of meaninglessness, lovelessness and uselessness, especially in pressure situations, can cause some human beings to gravitate toward self-destructive behavior, even when they know better. Yes; as suggested in the previous chapters, it is during the most arduous times that determination and self-motivation are supposed to kick in and keep you on the right path, yet for most ex-prisoners a certain fulfillment and extra validation can definitely be gotten from maintaining a close family relationship that may also help toward them making better decisions and maintaining the understanding that the people they love are just as affected by their actions as they themselves are, if not moreso. Being self-motivated is absolutely great;

being self-motivated and also having the presence and support of loved ones in your life is even better.

In other words, the flip side to Rule #2 is that ex-prisoners making it a point to have folks around them that give them real love, real support, and real understanding is a priceless component to any ex-prisoners' wellbeing, the same as it is to the average everyday person's wellbeing. The best case scenario for any man or woman that is fresh out of prison is for them to have a positive support system and/or family or true friends there for them, and not necessarily for financial support as much as mental and emotional support. A criminal-minded person who has spent time in prison could get out and somehow get filthy rich; if that person is not self-motivated to change and also does not have the presence and influence of those who truly care about their wellbeing in their life on a consistent basis, that person could still end up right back in trouble or back in prison despite having lots of money. Financially well-off criminal-minded people go to prison every day. I of all people understand just how important having money and being able to financially take care of yourself is when it comes to getting out of prison and being successful; I'm just saying that it is just as important that you have a mental and emotional support system as well. Like I've said, I have observed how loving family and friends helped to create that much needed security and positive support for many successful ex-prisoners. I have seen and experienced for myself how just having loved ones that communicate and come to visit is very therapeutic for those who are incarcerated. The key with this particular rule, however, is to make sure that you choose to stay close to and associate with those who *truly* love and care for you and not the so-called friends and associates or even family that really don't mean you any good and won't be of a positive help to your new mentality and ex-prisoner situation. It will be totally up to you to decipher, and decipher correctly, who really has your best interest at heart.

Also, I think that it is very important and proper for ex-prisoners to consider the hurt, harm and damage that has been done to their loved ones because of their criminal activity and incarceration and understand that it is only right that you attempt to make some reparations for that. Putting forth the effort to do this can sometimes be an arduous process, especially for those who have served really long terms of incarceration and who had children or spouses or parents who were really adversely affected by their situation, but for the most part all that those who *truly* care for you want is what is best for you. They will seriously want you to not ever have to go through incarceration again so they will try to help you make sure that doesn't happen if they can in whatever ways they can. By you adopting a mentality and lifestyle that is not 90%, not 95%, but 100% on the up and up and that's all about doing whatever you have to do to stay out of prison and succeed, you would be doing all that you could to repair the situation and you are showing and returning the love and dedication that they have shown you in the best way possible and giving them a return on their investment and belief in you. (Most prisoners and ex-prisoners do have people in their lives that love them and want to see them stay out of prison and succeed, so this advice applies to the vast majority of us.)

For those prisoners and ex-prisoners who want to be successful on the outside and who aren't fortunate enough to have supportive loved ones in their lives, that's no excuse and you're not off the hook; you still have to do what you have to do, for yourself. Don't use that as an excuse or reason to not take care of business and not do what's best for you. If you still remain dedicated and committed to personal change and success in spite of not initially having somebody being there to support you when you got out, you can still do just as well as the ex-prisoners who did have that initial support. You can eventually go on to create the loving supportive family or friend situation that you're missing in your life; if you don't already have it, creating it should be a major aspect of your plan for your future.

For any and all dedicated ex-prisoners: **Survival is a must and Success is the goal, and love and support is tremendously important to that process.** If you already have that love and support in your life, cling to it with all your might and consider yourself blessed. If you don't have it in your life, it would still be to your benefit to stay on the course of positive personal change and then one day create that supportive social situation for yourself, nurture it, reciprocate it and keep it as close to you as possible as much as possible. You staying close to those who truly care for you and you being family-oriented are the best things any ex-prisoner who is truly trying to change can do and it's in the best interest of everyone involved...especially you.

★ Rule #10 ★

Always Take the Time to Think Before You Act!

I think one of the simplest yet wisest pieces of advice I have ever been given in my life and that I in turn could ever give to other ex-prisoners, and anyone else for that matter, is to always try to think about your important actions and activities at least 3 times before you actually do them, and that if you make a habit of doing that you will consistently find that you make better decisions overall. "Think Before You Act" or "TBYA" as it's commonly referred to as is indeed a very cliché thing to say but is so, so important for all ex-prisoner's to remember *on a daily basis* when operating out in society.

Through conferring with many incarcerated criminals and ex-criminals about what their thought process was when they were engaging in criminal activity, I have found it to be a very common characteristic that they did not really give much deep thought to what they were doing and all the potential consequences associated with it. I know I didn't take the time to employ much deep thought myself when I was doing the criminal stuff I was doing. We didn't concentrate on what the long term results of our actions would be; somehow it didn't really cross our minds and if we had been in the habit of doing that we may never have even engaged in criminal activity in the first place. Taking sufficient time to think before you act is something that people have to be trained to do, so for most prisoners and ex-prisoners it will take some self-training to get into the habit of doing it. It's really just about making the observation that it's a wise thing to think heavily about your actions and the consequences thereof and then making it a point to practice doing it every time you are getting ready to make a decision to do something, whatever that "something" might be.

Really, extensive beforehand thinking before you act is the main aspect of planning as talked about in Rule #5, but it goes even beyond when you as an ex-prisoner are preparing your long-term plans because it is something you need to do even when no long-term planning is involved or necessary. It definitely is a practice that needs to become an everyday practice because we all know that in life almost anything can happen at the drop of a hat and at times it is necessary for us to make important split-second decisions; these are some of the times when having a developed habit of pausing for a few minutes to thoroughly think about what you are getting ready to do and the consequences thereof is invaluable. **The more thought and consideration that goes into a decision the more likely that decision will be the right one.**

Thinking before you act is simply about making sure that you are seeing and understanding your situations, issues and problems clearly before making your choices and decisions. Life is all about solving problems and getting over obstacles and it's been said that no one can ever correctly address and/or solve a problem that they are having unless they are able to first thoroughly analyze that problem, which requires that extensive beforehand "thinking". It's about the consideration of your choices and the costs and benefits of each possible choice. As I see it, the process to TBYA is 6 fold: Focusing clearly on the problem; Deciding upon your goal; Mentally or physically listing all of the possible choices that you could potentially make; Considering the costs and benefits of each potential choice; Making the decision that will enable you to reach your goal; and Evaluating your decision. Of course we all know that, generally speaking, the best choices are the ones where the benefits to you greatly outnumber or outweigh the costs but many times we engender less than what we wanted and sometimes even the direct opposite of what we would prefer and subsequently end up feeling really bad simply because we did not take the usually small amount of time that is necessary to critically think about what we were doing before we proceeded; it's called regret. When folks make it a habit to think before they act they typically live with a lot less trouble and a lot less regret which makes for a more fulfilled and satisfactory existence, and who doesn't want that? I believe that most all ex-prisoners not only want that, they *need* that.

   Like most of the other principles in this guidebook, thinking before you act is all about self-regulation. It can be explained to you what you should do but no one can force you to do it. It's not something that anybody else will be able to do for you either; you have to do it for yourself the same way that you have to employ self-discipline and personal responsibility and a good work ethic for yourself. It requires patience as well; the statement "Haste Makes Waste" is so true in the sense that hasty decisions almost never result in the best outcome. Making hasty decisions usually means wasted time, wasted energy, and wasted resources because there are almost always undesirable consequences to follow and corrections that will have to be made. Ex-prisoners should know this better than anyone, so to all ex-prisoners I simply say this: Unless you want to risk repeating the past and the "waste" of your life's precious time that occurred when you were sitting in prison and going through all the trials and tribulations that were the consequences of your actions, it would be in your best interest to always remember to think, think, think before you act and begin practicing that as soon as possible and seek to make that practice a never-ending habit of yours.

Victim Reconciliation and Forgiveness

The main focus of this guidebook, which as I've said I've tried to keep as simplified and as general as I could, is about what it will take for any and all ex-prisoners and ex-criminals who have ever served substantial amounts of time in prison anywhere in the world to make it on the outside after they have been released. Within the Rules of this guidebook I did not delve into all of the many aspects of victim reconciliation and forgiveness that most if not all ex-prisoners should engage in but I would be remiss if I did not point out that these are 2 *very* important facets of successful reentry as well. They are just as significant as any of the 10 Rules. It's very important for those who have committed crimes to identify and acknowledge *all* their victims, whether it was 1 or more individuals or a whole community that was victimized, and seek to analyze, recompense and come to positive terms with that on a personal level. (I do not think that any crime that is committed that especially involves a guilty person going to prison can be totally victimless, even if the only victims are the guilty person's own family members or loved ones who suffered because of their incarceration and absence. As far as I have seen there are not many "victimless crime" exceptions to the rule.) It is also just as important for you to forgive yourself and anyone else whom you feel has wronged you in the past; **forgiveness is the exitway out of most human self-defeating life cycles and before you can truly move forward anew you must embrace forgiveness of yourself and forgiveness of others.**

As talked about in Rule #9 in specific respect to reconciliation with family and loved ones that were adversely affected by your incarceration, it is very important and proper for you to consider the hurt, harm and damage that has been done to others because of the choice you made to engage in whatever criminal activity you were engaged in and understand that it is only right that you attempt to make some reparations for that. You may have officially "paid your debt to society" by doing time in prison and completing your sentence but you being locked up did not necessarily reverse whatever damage you may have done or whatever pain you may have caused to certain other persons and/or communities that were affected by your actions. It's very important that you see and understand the social and moral components involved in successful reentry and engage in some sort of direct victim reconciliation when and if at all possible.

Truly forgiving ourselves and others is many times the 1 thing many folks claim they just can't or won't do. Yes; forgiveness of yourself and others can often open up a big can of worms because it involves facing up to your own misdeeds and possibly extinguishing some very deep feelings you have for some other people but it offers you the opportunity to emotionally wipe the slate clean in order to be able to try all over again and be successful. Victim reconciliation is for the benefit of the victims but forgiving is something that you have to do for *you*, not for anyone else. Though you forgiving others does benefit them, that is not the main reason you need to do it. You *have* to forgive so that you can have inner peace and this means getting rid of any excess emotional baggage that has been weighing you down and holding you back so that you can be free to do and be whatever you need to, and like mostly everything else, it will more than likely be a process. You may have to work long and hard to heal your own wounds and make peace with your own past misdeeds and the misdeeds of others but if you commit yourself to an ongoing sincere healing process then true and real forgiveness of yourself and others *is* possible.

All in all, for the ex-prisoner, what generally applies here is this: **The best way to reconcile for your past criminal misdeeds and/or mistakes is for you to employ true forgiveness and get out of prison and not commit any more crimes and be a positive and responsible contributor to society.** If you are able to do more than that and can go above and beyond that reconciliation threshold where specific victims of your crime(s) are concerned then by all means I strongly encourage you to enthusiastically pursue doing that, but if not then rest assured that by you making the decision to be dedicated to changing yourself for the better and by becoming truly "successful" after prison you have done the best thing that you could possibly have done not only for yourself but for whomever was victimized by your criminal activity as well as the larger society. It's all about reconciling and reconciliation is about giving back; giving back to your victims, giving back to your family, giving back to your community, and giving back to yourself. It's what all ex-prisoners have a solemn duty to do, if you ask me. Putting together this guide to try and help other ex-prisoners find true meaning and success on the outside is one of my own ways of giving back and hopefully it will be of aid to you in that process and journey towards building that successful life on the outside. If you take heed to the 10 Rules and follow the advice herein, I, Richard Bovan, a truly reformed and successful ex-prisoner, can personally guarantee you that it will.

Other Recommended Readings For Ex-Prisoners

Cooked: From the Streets to the Stove, from Cocaine to Foie Gras by Jeff Henderson

How to Do Good After Prison: A Handbook for Successful Reentry by Michael B. Jackson

Getting Out & Staying Out: A Black Man's Guide to Success After Prison by Demico Boothe

Making Good: How Ex-Convicts Reform & Rebuild Their Lives by Shadd Maruna

Prisoners Once Removed: The Impact of Incarceration and Reentry on Children, Families, and Communities by Jeremy Travis and Michelle Waul

Other Recommended Readings For Ex-Prisoners

When Prisoners Come Home: Parole and Prisoner Reentry by Joan Petersilia

But They All Come Back: Facing the Challenges of Prisoner Reentry by Jeremy Travis

Barriers to Reentry? The Labor Market for Released Prisoners in Post-Industrial America by Shawn Bushway, Michael A. Stoll, David F. Weiman

Criminal Reform: Prisoner Reentry into the Community by Quintan B. Mallenhoff

When Prisoners Return: Why We Should Care and How You and Your Church Can Help by Pat Nolan, Chuck Colson

We're All Doing Time: A Guide to Getting Free by Bo Lozoff, The Dalai Lama

Lightning Source UK Ltd.
Milton Keynes UK
UKOW03f0732291213

223687UK00016B/1021/P